To Jackie ad Mardy —
Some songs of an old
and fading way of life —

Gene Ch Autry

November 1992

Nights under a Tin Roof

Recollections of a Southern Boyhood

by

James A. Autry

Introduction by John Mack Carter
Graphic Design — Stacey Locke

YOKNAPATAWPHA PRESS
OXFORD, MISSISSIPPI

ii

Published by Yoknapatawpha Press, Inc.
P.O. Box 248, Oxford MS 38655

Copyright © 1983 by James A. Autry

Library of Congress Catalogue Card Number 83-50002.

ISBN 0-916242-26-9

Second Printing, May 1984 Third printing, Sept. 1985

Printed in the United States of America

DEDICATION

In Memory Of

my mother,

Ruth Edna Eubanks Autry McKinstry

my father,

Ewart Arthur Autry

my brother and best friend,

Ewart Ronald Autry

◆ ◆ ◆

Mother painted with oils and watercolors and ink and vegetable dyes on canvas and wood and glass and metal and anything at hand a hundred scenes of her Mississippi childhood.

Dad preached in more country churches at more revival meetings and more weddings and more funerals than anyone could count, and he wrote such sentences as "It was a day of wind and rain in the valley of the little Tippah" in thousands of stories about his Mississippi homeland.

And Ronald came out of Mississippi into a fast world of news journalism and still wrote stories and poems about all of that old life which follows us everywhere, and sang gospel music and never lost touch, and before he died, encouraged me to finish this book.

CONTENTS

◆ ◆ ◆

FOREWORD

When I first read some of these pieces to a fellow Mississippian, a writer now living in Virginia, she said, "I'm astonished that you look back with such benevolence, with no bitterness."

It was then I realized I was not sticking to the mode of the expatriate Southerner who tends to pass judgment on "the magnolia mentality" or to scorn the southern social structure.

Well, I thought, there's nothing I can add to what's been said already. And if there were I still wouldn't do it here. Not in these recollections, because they were not seen with the adult eye or filtered through the sensitivities of the educated. All that stuff came later, found its way into prose now tucked under papers in old college footlockers or into speeches made in the sixties and seventies.

Instead, here are the forties and fifties, not as an examination of forces shaping the South, rather as forces shaping me. Personally. Just me. Mississippi boy, adolescent, teenager.

Maybe I'll take my turn at all that professional southern introspection one of these days. Certainly it's in me, but it would not be, were there not also a nurturing presence from an earlier, gentler time.

I suppose I've needed for many years to express that earlier time in a form which could somehow paint the place and character and people and language with the generosity and gratitude I feel. But until 1977 I was unable to come even close to doing it.

Then I heard James Dickey reading from his own work one evening; it was so powerful, so full of what I wanted to create that I returned to my hotel and scribbled seven short poems before the night was over. They were terrible but represented a change of form and, more important, a change in my thinking. For that I thank James Dickey, whose work sets a wonderful standard for us all.

I'm not sure my early poems were poetry, and some people have asked if the work in this book is really poetry. Each reader can answer for himself. I call these writings "pieces" because their shape comes to me as stories and then as pieces of a larger story.

Their form began to emerge in 1980 when Betty Sue Flowers, friend and mentor, scholar, professor, and poet, took it upon herself to help my understanding of, thus my writing of, poetry. We met at the Aspen Institute in 1980, and Betty Sue has carried on a mostly long-distance seminar with me ever since, a gift I can never repay.

As for making a book, the thought never occurred to me until late one night in Oxford, Mississippi, when I ended up at the faculty house of Willie Morris who, at the time, was writer in residence at Ole Miss. He read one of his essays, later to be published in *Terrains of the Heart.*

"Your turn to read something," he said, much to the disappointment, I'm sure, of a couple of students who had been swaying with his every word. I had some poems in my briefcase, and after I read two, Willie pointed to me and said, "Come home, Autry. Come home and publish."

That late-night performance led to a meeting with Larry Wells who listened to a few poems, read others for himself, then wrote a letter saying he would like to publish a book of my poetry. Soon after, I met his wife, Dean Faulkner Wells who told me that my work reminded her of her childhood near Oxford. Then it unfolded, as these spiritual connections seem always to do, that several of these poems were written about the same places, the same people, the same church experiences — for her grandfather (mentioned by name in one poem) and my father were songleader and preacher, respectively, in the same church at the same time.

By my romantic vision, that coincidence makes this book a project of the spirit. Nothing less.

Throughout it all, I have been supported by loved ones, family and friends too numerous to list. But I love you all and I thank you all.

A few words about the photographs. They come from three sources: the Library of Congress, the Mississippi Department of History and Archives, and family photo albums. These pictures are here to complement and not specifically to illustrate the poetry; enjoy them as another artistic expression of many of the same themes and events.

◆ ◆ ◆

J.A.A.
Van Meter, Iowa 1983

INTRODUCTION

by John Mack Carter

New York, N.Y.
November 1, 1982

When I first came north many years ago to work in New York City, I didn't understand how much I didn't know. I plunged into this new world happily and confidently, with no fear of the new experiences and no envy of any person. After a few months one of my new-made friends, a native New Yorker only a few years older but with a lifetime of metropolitan sophistication, confided, "I envy you. You know who you are."

I recall that comment because I remember my puzzlement. I had always known who I was. Yet here was a woman who seemingly had the answer to every question about the city and its celebrities as well as a world across the ocean I hadn't even seen, yet she envied my native knowledge of self.

This is why when Jim Autry told me he was writing these poems, I knew exactly what it was he was inspired to share with us. I suggest that this shared experience can be a thing of great value.

Jim and I have worked as contemporaries in the same profession of editing magazines. And we both have come the long way to New York to do it. But the instant I met Jim I knew that we were bound in a kinship that only could be formed by nights and days "under a tin roof."

Ours was a time of the South that produced writers, possibly because it was a time that promised to go on forever. We were living in an endless summer that owed nothing to tomorrow, and we were bound by neither urgency nor despair. The swollen sun was all the promise we needed.

Most of that South is gone, and the new South of progress and change — better in so many ways — may not provide these songs again.

For all of us lucky enough to know who we are, and those of us still eager to find out, Jim has laid this roof of tin.

◆ ◆ ◆

I. Rhythms

· · ·

Nights Under a Tin Roof

I

When the fire still sends its yellow light from the bank of coals
is best
before the cold pushes us under the quilts
while the frost is still invisible in the air
And we can look up to the uneven planks fifteen years from the sawmill
and still not painted
and make things and faces in the wood grain
and be scared and laugh

> *You boys settle down in there*
> *We'll be getting up 'round here*
> *in a few minutes*

But we wouldn't
as we didn't stop peeking the cracks at Allie Jo and Mae Beth

> *You see Allie Jo's pants*
> *You didn't neither*
> *Did too when she blew the lamp*

Peeking those same cracks that let the wasps through
that always needed stuffing with paper.

Uncle Virgil covered the kitchen cracks with wallpaper from the catalogue but
mice ate the wheat paste making tunnels like moles
and Uncle Vee mashed them with his fist and pulled them through
so the kitchen wall had little holes in the printed roses where a tunnel
stopped
And the rest of the rolls are wrapped in newspaper under the bed
because it might work better someday with another paste

> *Now you boys don't pee off the porch*
> *do your business under the chinaberry tree*

Those same cracks that let the smells through the floor
like the time Aunt Callie put out the ant poison and the rats got it on their feet
then licked them and died under the house

You ain't smelled stink till you smelled
a old wolf rat dead with the poison

And who had to rake them out with a stick
who was little enough to squeeze under the floor scared of snakes
and gagging with the smell

Take em yonder to the gulley boys
mind that lye on your hands

II

When the rain plays different notes
high near the peak and low in the middle
is best
When the thunder is far off down the Tippah bottom
and the wind is settled to breezes
and early before light we hear the back door and Uncle Vee's boots
and the pine fire in the stove and the lid on the salt box
and the pot boiling

Boys don't put so much sugar
in that coffee

But there was always the lightning when it struck the cat
right out of Jimmie Lee's arms and burned out the screen door
and killed the cat and only knocked Jimmie Lee down

Thank you Lord for that sign

And we can't go out in it especially under the trees
or go near the stove or windows

Stay on the bed and don't touch the floor boys
and don't bounce

and only the girls can use the slop jar except when it lightnings
and we always need it then

Well use the slop jar boys
but you'll have to take it out

When the dark comes with the afternoon clouds
and we hear lightning striking the pines on hickory nut hill
and the air whispers like God shushing everybody before the thunder
we try not to jump when it comes
and Aunt Callie brings tea cakes from the kitchen
round and sugary and crumbly with burned bottoms
and chewy with thick middles
and cow's milk to dip them

> *Don't drip on the quilt boys*

And Uncle Vee crumbles corn bread in blue john milk
and rocks and looks out the window

> *It'll be dry 'nough to pick up potaters boys*
> *if the lightnin' didn't scare the life*
> *outta preacher mule*

III

When a whip-poor-will sets in the yard and calls another in the garden
is best
and we sleep on top of the covers
when the windows are propped open
and balls of last year's cotton are wired on the screens with hair pins
keeping out the flies
And we hear Uncle Vee hiking there the walker hounds
to the bottom below the old place

> *Just listen at the window boys*
> *you'll hear the hounds good as me*

And Aunt Callie washes a block of ice from the sawdust pile
and puts it in a pitcher of cistern water

> *Don't play around that cistern boys*
> *we'll never see you again*

That's when the snakes come out
like the copperhead that bit Aunt Callie getting up the cows
and Uncle Vee tore his shirt for her heel
and we ran all the way to Cousin Verdell's who had a Dodge

> *Knowed somethin' was wrong boys*
> *when I heard your feet slappin' the ground*

When the night doesn't cool down
Uncle Vee puts his feet in a dishpan of water
and Miss Ann fans with the big palm leaf James Edward brought from Hawaii
before he got killed on the destroyer in the Solomons
after Becky won the Miss USS Edward Turner contest
and his dog Frisco just went off and died

> *Let him go boys*
> *he don't want you to find him*

Uncle Vee doesn't sell the place
but he'll let me put a house on it someday
with a tin roof

Best roof in the world if you nail it right boys
take a twister

And it keeps the place dry
and turns away the summer sun
and sends back the fireplace heat through the winter cracks
And holds everything together through the storms

◆ ◆ ◆

Communication

Now we dial the phone
but Aunt Callie still yells into it
and ends every sentence with a question mark
as if she can't believe that all her words
can get through those little wires

But back then we stepped out and pointed our voices
across the hills

>*Whooooeeee*

It would follow the bottoms and up the next hill
and in a few minutes
it would come back from Cousin Lester

>*Whooooeeee*

When there was trouble
Uncle Vee would blow the fox horn
or ring the dinnerbell
and someone with a car would come
not knowing the problem but that we needed a car.

When Uncle Vee yelled or blew the horn
there was a message to send

>*Don't you boys be out there*
>*yellin' up somebody*
>*'less you got somethin' they need to know*

But we'd yell
and the old folks would know we were just yelling
and let it go
our high voices somehow falling short of the next hill
the dogs not even coming from under the porch.

Weeks would pass without a real yell
then it would roll up the hill from Cousin Lester's

>*Whoooooeeeeee*

And Uncle Vee would step out on the porch
and cup his hands and answer
and turn his head and listen
nodding at the message I could never understand.

It's how we heard Cousin Lottie got snake bit
and James Louis came back from the Pacific

It's how the fox hunts were arranged
and the hog killings set

They yelled about babies born and people cured
about fires and broken bones and cows loose and dogs lost
the words always short and spaced
for the distance they had to travel.

Now there are the wires
and Aunt Callie still yells for the distance
and looks at the phone
holding it so her eyes can aim the words
through the instrument and across the hills
where they are to go

◆ ◆ ◆

Cotton Poison

We called it cotton poison
and its smell became good
drifting across the roads with the dust
lying in clouds on the July fields
Because underneath
we knew it was killing the weevil
and the weevil had killed us
every year before

Until the poison came
the cotton was armpit high and good
but inside the weevil was doing his work
Until the poison came
we carried barlow knives to the fields
and mashed the weevil from the split boll
hoping one hard death would scare the others
and heal the cotton
Until the poison came
it was God's will and the weevil was his

Now the poison drifts with the tractor dust
and the soldiers come home from Okinawa and the Bulge
ride into the night and jump in the river
the dust floating from their overalls
and laugh themselves dry
thinking of a bale to the acre
Because they beat the weevil like they beat the Nazis and Japs
and all their daddies could do was pray

◆ ◆ ◆

The Snakes

There were snakes
my god there were bad snakes
but we didn't see all that many
except in Aunt Callie's imagination
under every log and in every brushpile

> *Now you chirren watch*
> *you'll step on a snake*

We knew them all
the copperhead/rattlesnake pilot/highland moccasin
(all the same snake)
plus the gentleman rattlesnake
who would always rattle before he struck
and the treacherous cottonmouth
hidden beside the path waiting for the chance to bite not run

> *Cottonmouths got to discharge that poison*
> *so they got to bite somethin' or somebody*

And there were copperbellies not poison but mean
and after Uncle Vee killed them
he pushed their heads into the soft mud with a stick
deep so half the snake was in the hole

> *It's a sign our family*
> *killed the snake*

And there were good snakes especially the king snakes

> *You ought to see him kill a bad 'un boys*
> *wrap hisself around that other'n*
> *and squeeze him to death*

But we killed them all
because a snake was a snake

> *Well I couldn't tell, Uncle Vee*
> *they all look bad*

There were spreading adders that puffed and hissed and acted mean
but couldn't hurt you
and rat snakes and bull snakes and hog nose snakes
and chicken snakes that ate our eggs and baby chicks
and when you reached into a nest on a high shelf in the chicken house
an old settin' hen might peck you

or it could be a chicken snake
so sometimes eggs in a high nest would go rotten
because we'd all think the next day's cousin would get them.

There were blue racers and black racers
and one time rabbit hunting
Uncle Vee and Cousin Lester saw a racer and kicked it
like when they were boys
and it curled up in a ball
and the other one kicked it high in the trees
it staying in a tight little ball
then both running for it and Cousin Lester kicking Uncle Vee
and they both falling in the leaves

> *Won't that kill the racer, Uncle Vee?*
> *Sure will*

And glass snakes that broke into pieces when you hit them
yes, really into sections
each one wiggling on its own

> *You leave him alone boys*
> *he'll get back together*
> *no matter how far you scatter them pieces*
> *take one a mile away he'll get back together*

One day on the path to the spring
Jimmy Lee and I saw a hog nose snake swallowing a toad
so we watched him do it
throwing his jaw all out of joint
the toad kicking his legs and hopping
making the snake's head jump off the ground
like a snake with hind legs in its head
then when the toad was inside
we killed the snake and cut him open
and the toad hopped away.

But the mean snakes were moccasins
even the un-poison ones
the brown water snakes at the swimming hole
that come toward you with open mouths hissing

> *They got a nest here somewhere boys*

and we always argued whether they could bite you under water
and we never found out.

After Aunt Callie got bit by the copperhead
all the men went hunting for bad snakes
with hoes and some shotguns
They turned over logs and whistled at brushpiles

saying a long straight whistle will bring them out
and at the end had killed hundreds of snakes
bad and good
and we measured the longest ones
and some of the boys skinned them for belts.

Then we didn't worry about snakes for a while
and hoped maybe they were all killed off

> *They'll be back boys*
> *they were in the Garden of Eden*
> *and they'll be back here*

◆ ◆ ◆

Seasons Came with Food

I

Seasons came with food
not the other way around
certainly not with rain or winds or sun
or any weather at all
But when onion sets and potato cuts went in
it was February and the red sand soil
was cold under the fingernails
and our noses ran

> *Now you chirrun*
> *keep those coats buttoned*

Then it was mustard greens
we sowed in patches
to mix with wild poke salad
or collards that would take the frost.

When the water warmed we'd fish
for lazy willow cats hungry after the winter
or blues or jugheads or the quick channels
caught on set hooks and trot lines
run late at night in a boat
or barefoot along the slick bank
fighting mosquitos and scared of cottonmouths

> *Don't step over a log*
> *you can't see the other side of, boys*

Girls picked dewberries low on the ground
and somebody would make a pie

> *I declare you chirrun*
> *eat yourself sick*
> *if I let you*

Aunt Callie would can the rest
sweating over the steaming pots
with summer almost here
and the garden in and the greens up

> *A mess of greens and a pone of bread*
> *won't be long now*

Then it seemed something all the time
squash and new potatoes and green onions
the meals getting good and the canning hotter.

II

There came the day when
we soaked rags in coal oil
and tied them on our wrists and ankles

> *Them chiggers love blackberry bushes*
> *better'n I love blackberries*

And we'd fill our one gallon buckets
with the dark berries staining our hands
and chiggers getting past the coal oil
with the wasps nests and the yellow jackets
and always the snakes

> *Copperheads love to lie up*
> *in the shade of those blackberries*
> *so make plenty of noise chirrun*

Then everything was easier
with only some wild plums to pick
and potatoes turned over by a plow
looking rich and good in the dirt
and stored in piles in a dark place
under the house

> *Now don't you boys whine about spiders*
> *just mind your business and come back*
> *for another load*

We ate peas and corn and tomatoes and
greens and onions and cornbread
and drank buttermilk
when the cows got into bitterweed
and the sweet milk tasted bad
And when everybody was full of watermelon
Aunt Callie made preserves from the rinds
and ground and chopped squash and cucumbers
and pickled little hot peppers
to pour over the greens and sop with bread.

III

By September the woods smelled of muscadines
and we picked them by the gallon
shaking trees and laughing when they rained on us
then finding them among the leaves

> *I declare you chirrun eat more*
> *than you put in the bucket*

Their seed sacks shot into our mouths
as we sucked the musky hulls
And Aunt Callie canned some and made jelly
and preserves and acid drink

> *Now I tell you that ain't wine*
> *and I don't want to hear no more about it*

and if we were good
fried pies crisp outside
where they almost burned in the skillet
and sometimes skim cream
to put on a cobbler
we'd eat in front of a young fall fire

> *You spoil those chirrun to death*

And we'd clean our guns
and talk about deer and rabbits and ducks and quail
and laugh at who'd miss
and who'd have to clean the rabbits

> *Worse smell*
> *Lord I'd rather skin a skunk*

Or Uncle Vee would get the smokehouse
ready for the hog killing

> *Soon's we're sure the weather'll stay cold.*

IV

Still later when ice was on the ponds
with the salt box full
and jars on the shelves
the colors of their contents tempting us
the comfort of it would settle upon us
and some morning soon after Christmas
before a pine fire
Uncle Vee would be looking out the window

> *Think we'll put the potaters*
> *between the fruit trees this year boys*
> *might's well use that ground*

then one day it wouldn't seem so cold
and we'd hear the gee and haw
and the chains on the single tree
and the soft tearing of the new ground
over the plow

◆ ◆ ◆

After a season of planting and weeding and harvesting, a woman of Greene county, Georgia, shows off her canning and cupboard in 1941. Photo from the Library of Congress.

Left: Father and son sharpen their mower on a rainy day in Carroll county, Georgia, 1941. Below: Father and daughter with a load of cotton in Alabama, 1933. Right: Wearing a bonnet against the North Carolina sun, 1940. Photos: Library of Congress.

*Left and Right:
Slopping the
hogs, a daily
chore leading
to that
inevitable
time when a fat
sow is killed
and butchered.
Photo: Mississippi
Department of
Archives and History,
Florence Mars
collection.
Below: Sorghum-
making with
a mule turning
the mill.
Photo: Library
of Congress*

Nothing defined
life's rhythms so
much as
the growing
season. Planting,
tilling,
weeding, and
harvesting were
the events
which shaped life
from the time
the spring
sun began to warm
the soil.
Here a Georgia
farmer
plows a garden
with his mule
while his
son follows and
carefully
drops peas into
the new ground.
At right, a
Mississippi
farm hand chops
cotton under
a relentless sun.
Photos: Library
of Congress

All over the south
schools closed
at cotton-
picking time,
and the children
went to the
fields, dragging
their 11-foot
sacks between
the rows. The
children above
were photographed
in Arkansas in
about 1940. Below,
the cotton
wagons gather at
the gin in Clarke
county, Georgia
in 1940. Photos:
Library of Congress.
At right, voters
in Mississippi
consider the merits
of keeping Jim.
Photo: Mississippi
Department of Archives
and History,
Florence Mars
collection.

KEEP JIM

EASTLAND
U. S. SENATOR

In between numbers they sipped moonshine or sucked at beer bottles then kicked off the beat for another tune. It happened in national guard armories and at street dances. The band above is Cajun, playing for a fais-dodo in Louisiana. The street dancers are in the same town, circa 1938. Photos: Library of Congress. (Also overleaf) Below, Mississippi men gather on the square for first Monday business. Photo: Mississippi Department of Archives and History, Florence Mars collection.

Buzzards

I

Buzzards would stack
a hundred at a time
the highest fly specks in a hot summer sky
and circle something dead
And we'd wonder what it was
and talk about walking to it
through the woods
sighting on the stack of buzzards
until we'd arrive underneath
and there it would be
whatever it was
Dead and big
we knew it would be big

II

But we did it one time
making two buzzards fly
filling the air
with their awful smell
and it was only a rabbit
all those buzzards for one dead rabbit
Were they waiting their turn
up there a mile
turning turning never flapping a wing
not a feather
riding on some wind we couldn't see or feel
and waiting a turn
on one dead rabbit?
Were dead things in such short supply?

III

It was the depression maybe
no money and no dead things
A lot of buzzards
with not much to do
We would watch them for hours
sometimes instead of chopping cotton
stopping in the field
leaning on a hoe
lying by the big cedar

◆ ◆ ◆

Things Done Right

I

Now there are ruts in the floor
where Aunt Callie rocks with a morning cup of coffee
and warms her feet at a gas heater
whose black pipe shoots into the old chimney
where the fireplace had been.

But back when the ruts were young
the first sounds of morning were ashes being stirred
the thump of fresh logs
the pop of pine kindling in the cook stove
the quiet talk of the grownups
and the radio with its thin and fuzzy hillbilly music

> *How many biscuits can you eat*
> *this mornin' this mornin'*
> *How many biscuits can you eat*
> *this evenin' this evenin'*
> *How many biscuits can you eat*
> *Pillsbury biscuits can't be beat*
> *this mornin' this evenin' right now*

and the weather reports Uncle Vee always turned up.
We'd hear him walk to the door
and know he was looking at the sky

> *Don't care what the weather man says*
> *gonna rain this afternoon*

Then the radio would go down
and Aunt Callie and Uncle Vee would have their quiet time
and talk about the day
and he would say where he planned to work
and she would talk about washing or canning
or sewing or working the garden
and they would decide what we children would do
We'd hear the hiss of something frying
and wonder what it was before we could smell it
salt meat or bacon or maybe country ham

> *Better call those chirrun*
> *biscuits goin' in*

And the smells settling into the whole house
all the way under the covers
would help us wake up

II

Even in the hot of July
the cook stove was fired
and Aunt Callie baked biscuits every meal
using her big wooden dough bowl of flour
and pinching in lard and squeezing in buttermilk
working it only with her hands
then lifting the dough and rolling it out
cutting the biscuits with a baking powder can.

And there might be fried pies
sealed with a fork dipped in water
and pressed evenly along a crescent edge
Or a fruit pie with a tall crust
scalloped by the quick and perfect twists
of a buttered thumb and forefinger
Between meals Aunt Callie kept the stove hot
simmering a slow pot of string beans and salt meat
boiling water for dishes
heating irons on the day after wash day
How she would sweat in her loose wash dress
ironing everything from the clothesline
sprinkling with her hand dripping from a pan of water
sometimes pressing a cedar cutting under cloth
to make a pair of church trousers smell better
working fast before her iron cooled down
licking her finger and sizzling it against the iron
to check its hotness
as it sat on an old coffee can lid
at the end of the ironing board
And leaving no piece of cloth untouched
dish towels, sheets, tablecloths and wash rags
overalls and work shirts
which would be sweat wet and wrinkled in five minutes
even undershorts
and always making us boys change everything everyday

> What if you's to be taken to the clinic
> or somethin'
> you want to be dirty?

And folding everything on shelves and in drawers
as if they would never be touched
but be looked at and admired
and passed on
by some work clothes inspector.

On other days she churned
humming hymns to the wet rhythm of the dasher

the kitchen filled with bowls and buckets of milk
clabber or blue john or buttermilk
with cheesecloth keeping out the flies

III

And Uncle Vee was the same
the way he hitched his mule
and plowed his garden
geeing and hawing up and down the rows
always in the same direction
The way he put in his potatoes and onion sets
then unhitched the mule and fed and watered him
and always told the same stories

> *One time this old man asked his mule*
> *you want any more oats old boy*
> *and the mule lifted his tail*
> *and the sound came out his rear*
> *ffffeeewwwww*

and laughed and shook his head and slapped his knee
and said the punch line again

> *ffffeeewwwww*

The way he measured two double handfuls of shorts
for each hog and mixed it with slop from the table
as if the hogs might not eat it done wrong
And in the evening after supper
laid a fire with pine knots and split wood
so it burned with one match
and never had to be stoked a second time
then sat with a cup of coffee
and always worked on something
maybe patching a stew pan with screws and a washer
or rigging a trotline or cleaning his double barrel
or sharpening his barlow knife
spitting on a whetrock
and drawing the blade toward him and away
and testing its sharpness against the hairs on his arm

> *Most dangerous thing in the world, boys*
> *is a dull knife*
> *cut you faster'n a sharp one*

and while Aunt Callie snapped peas or shelled butterbeans
he would peel an apple
putting his barlow to it and turning the apple
so the peel came in one long spiral

stretching halfway to the floor

>*You ain't peeled an apple*
>*till you can do that, boys*

And when we tried it
then and much, much later
the peel always broke and fell
and the apple never tasted the same

◆ ◆ ◆

Nigger Wedding

When we had a '37 Ford coupe
but most people were in mule and wagon
and everybody was in town to do
first Monday business
I heard it from some of the little boys
who hung around the croquet court
on the courthouse lawn

> *Two niggers want to get married*
> *and nobody'll do it*

Uncle Vee made me walk with him
slowly like there wasn't any reason to go
and there was a crowd around the niggers
but nobody was saying anything

> *Is they a judge or somebody*
> *to do a ceremony?*

The man was in his soldier suit
with a big 2 on the shoulder
because the second army headquarters
was in Memphis

> *I got a license*
> *and we don't have much time*
> *but the clerk he won't do it*

Some laughed and some said
why would they bother
then someone saw Brother Thompson

> *There's a preacher, boy*
> *he could do it*

Brother Thompson brought his Bible
and they stood under the trees
on the croquet court

> *Make 'em jump over a broom Brother Thompson*
> *that's all they need*

The man held the woman's hand
and Brother Thompson said the words
and everybody was quiet
and when some of the boys laughed

they got kicked or ears or hair yanked.

Then they were married
and there was laughing and clapping

> *Kiss her boy*
> *let's see you kiss her*

But the man laughed and wouldn't do it
even when Brother Thompson said
salute the bride.
One man came with the janitor's broom
from the courthouse

> *Hell, make 'em jump a broom*
> *that's how my granddaddy married niggers*

But Uncle Vee and some other men
talked him out of it
and everybody began to go on
about their business

> *How much we owe you preacher?*
> *Dollar'll do*

They said much obliged
and drove off in an old truck
and some of the men started a croquet game
and others shook their heads and laughed a while.

◆ ◆ ◆

Scenes of Courtship

I

They said she was an old crazy girl
who lived at the bottom of the hill
and we always honked when we went by
thinking of all the things we'd do with her
if only we had the nerve to stop

>   *Blow the whistle Junior*
>   *then step on it*

And we'd hònk at any time of night
stepping on it before her father
could get to the window

>   *He tole the sheriff*
>   *he was gonna shoot anybody who honked*

On Saturdays when the crop was laid by
we'd put on khakis and a white shirt
hitched up two turns on the sleeve
our arms white above the sun browned hands
and we'd cock our elbows out the window
looking over our shoulders
sucking a match stick toothpick
and make the square slowly
but still spinning the tires on the turns
the white '46 Ford pickup washed with buckets from the creek
a white wall tire on the tailgate
and a skull turning knob on the steering wheel.
And we'd go to the dance at the national guard armory
and listen to Jimmy Deal and his Rythm Ranchers
and sip moonshine from fruit jars in paper sacks
and get brave enough to dance with country girls
because we thought they were easy
in their flour sack dresses
and their legs scratched from shaving with their daddy's razor

>   *Now we gotta go straight home*
>   *after the dance*

But we'd head for the moonlit cemetery
four in the pickup seat and always squeezing closer
when shadows moved among the stones

Start the motor
I know I saw somethin' that time

And our hands would fall in laps
and be pushed away
or our fingers would brush as if by accident
the soft bosom front of those flowered dresses
our khakis tightening with the intensity of that touch

I got my hand right on it Junior

II

But that was so much later
than when we courted at revival meetings
fanning through the singing and the preaching
every morning and every night
swimming in the afternoons
driving there in Winston's courting car
the '37 chevy truck with the cab cut off
open to the dust and gravel
taking a load to the creek and going back for more
jumping from the bank of the little Tobi Tubbi
named for an indian chief's wife
and the coldest creek in the country

Hey Winston dive on down
and bring us up some ice

And the girls would wear shorts over their bathing suits
some with the new elastic suits in light colors
and others in the old wool suits
that would get loose and sag open at the leg.
Someone would bring a watermelon from the creek
where it had been cooling
and we'd squirt the seeds from between our thumb and forefinger
until we were spotted
then jump in the Tobi Tubbi and wash them away

Y'all better come on
we gonna be late to revival

In the evening we wore
two toned cotton shirts starched
and we'd fan and sing and listen
and wait for the hayride to Mr. Bruce Wilford's melon patch

I bet you won't sit by Allie Jo
I bet you won't kiss her

III

When the big boys went off to the war
and came home in their uniforms
we'd hide in the bushes where they parked
and watch them press their girls against the car seat
or sometimes in the summer
lean them backwards against the fender

>*He put his hand*
>*up her sweater Junior*

while we only played spin the bottle
at birthday parties
and didn't press against anyone
and didn't have uniforms

IV

It was a sin for a Baptist to dance
so we went with Methodist girls
who taught us to slow dance and jitterbug

>*Hey look at old Junior*
>*do the dirty boogie*

Then dance on the Tippah river bridge
to music from the radio
in Ben Edwin McKinsey's daddy's '39 Pontiac coupe

>*Now if this runs the battery down*
>*y'all got to help me push her off*

Until one time
when Betty Sue Wilford fell off the bridge
and broke her arm and got scratched up
and Ben Edwin had to carry her to Oxford in the coupe
and the old people found out about the dancing
and made us pray for forgiveness
and Ben Edwin couldn't get the coupe any more

V

But later when Junior bought the pickup from his daddy
and fixed it up
we had four in the front seat every Saturday night
and parked at the cemetery
and sometimes one couple would get back in the bed

on some hay and an old quilt Junior kept in a tool box
the girls always afraid the other was watching

> *If they can see us*
> *Marianne will tell everybody in school*

Until one night after a dance at the Water Valley armory
when I couldn't go
Junior and Betty Vee Fox hit ice on the Tallahatchee bridge
And all we could do was put black borders
around their pictures in the year book
where Junior was handsomest and Betty Vee was wittiest

VI

Then everybody graduated and got jobs
or went to the army
and there was a lot of marrying
And those who went to college
came back every once in a while
but didn't want country girls any more
and would not be seen in a pickup truck

◆ ◆ ◆

II. People, Places, Happenings

...

Photo: Library of Congress

Grave Digger

His name is Otis Cox
and the graves he digs with a spade are acts of love.
The red clay holds like concrete
still he makes it give up a place
for rich caskets and poor
working with sweat and sand
in the springing tightness of his hair
saying that machine digging
don't seem right if you know
the dead person.
His pauses are slow as the digging
a foot always on the shovel.
Shaking a sad and wet face
drying his sorrow with a dust orange white handkerchief
he delivers a eulogy

Miz Ruth always gimme a dipper of water

Then among quail calls and blackeyed susans
Otis Cox shapes with grunt and sweat and shovel
a perfect work
a mystical place
a last connection with the living hand

◆ ◆ ◆

The Store

Up behind the store
doves roost in green kudzu
and niggers live in gray houses.
There we play in orange brown fields
between tall pines
quick as quail
running in black and white coveys
through boy high broom sedge.

Down in the summer dusty store yard
red mules suck green mossy water from wooden troughs
and men sit in caved cane chairs and suck wet peanuts from big orange drinks.
There we feel the mules' velvet gray noses
and pretend our light touch fingers are horseflies
tickling the long twitching ears.
Then scooping the vile water and flinging it at every close boy
we turn the dust to mud between our toes.

Inside the banana smelling store
men open Nehi belly washers and shake their heads about the weather
and women measure rat cheese and coal oil and softly pat new feed sack patterns.
There sitting on a floor shuffled thin by bare feet and brogans
we catch slow winged flies
and dash them into corner spiderwebs
watching their buzzing struggle until the quick step spider comes.
Then with tiny saving bites
we share a penny niggertoe
its white and chocolate melting sticky
onto all our hands.

◆ ◆ ◆

Cousin Verdell on Food

When I eat those drumsticks from some chicken
who never scratched the dirt
I think of Cousin Verdell's ideas about food

> *Best thing to eat*
> *is somethin' that'll eat*
> *somethin' else's droppin's*

And the thought of it made our mouths taste bad
and we figured Verdell was crazy

> *I tell you boys*
> *you think about it*

But we didn't want to
so we'd talk about fishing
and he'd talk about catfish

> *They eat dead stuff off the bottom*
> *I seen 'em eat manure*
> *and they absolutely the best tastin' fish*

Or we'd say we had to do chores
and he'd talk about pigs

> *Eat any damn thing*
> *eat they young'uns*
> *eat snakes*
> *eat all kinda slop*
> *and they absolutely the best meat*

There was no stopping him
until after the chickens

> *And chickens*
> *Boys they foller*
> *other animals 'round*
> *just to eat the corn outta they shit*
> *Hell they eat they own shit*
> *And what'd you rather eat than fried chicken?*

Verdell said God gave all those things a special organ
a purifying system
a way of taking what other creatures wasted
and turning it into something good.

But he wouldn't know what to say now
about a chicken who never scratched the dirt

◆ ◆ ◆

The Outhouse

I

It happens in places where they fold toilet paper
in little points
Where the seat is contoured
and the flush handle is from the modern museum
Where the tub is pastel
and the towels hang on heated bars
Where the sunlamps are on timers
and magnifying mirrors scissor out
to show the back of your head
That I think of all the terrors of the outhouse
on a dark and cold night
with wind bending the pines
with screech owls
with dogs howling in the bottom
and who knows what waiting
in that dark and putrid cavern below the splintery seat
maybe a new and unknown something
hatched from that awful murk
lying there or sliding or worming its way upward
waiting for that next soft bottom
to block its only view.
Or even things known and feared

> One time an old boy over'n Union county
> got bit right on the dingus
> by a black widder. Died.

II

We'd play so long and hard at the end of a day
we never wanted to stop

> Now if you boys have to do a job
> you better do it before dark

But sometimes we wouldn't
or we'd time it all wrong
or it would hit us after supper.
And how could the grownups tell?

> You better go on out there now
> you can't wait till mornin'

They always knew
and we couldn't undress for bed
until we took the coal oil lantern
and some pages from the catalog or newspaper
and after trying to get someone to come with us
just to stand outside
and after calling the dogs
who also seemed to know it was a wasted trip
whistled our way down the path
and into the shadowy drafty spidery three holer
talking loudly to no one
kicking the floor and seat
trying sometimes to squat balanced above the hole
so our bare skin would not be exposed to whatever there was
and finally
did our job (as Aunt Callie would say)
and made our way back
toward the lamp lit windows of the house

◆ ◆ ◆

Crow Killer

Why did he want to kill the crows
when he could talk to them
and call them up
and when they made him so happy
fighting owls and coming to his voice
when he created out of his own mouth
a battle
a mortal struggle
setting them against their old enemies?

But he killed them in a dozen clever ways
with a cow bell around his neck
and an old brown patchwork quilt over his back
crawling
on all fours among the cows
mocking their rhythm
swinging his head
ringing the bell
moving slowly toward the big beech tree
where the crows perched outsmarting everybody in the county
except Mr. C. W. the crow killer
who rose up from under the patchwork
with his double barrel
and got two
their awkward black bodies falling among the real cows
who hardly jumped when Mr. C.W. pulled the triggers.

But his favorite was the fight
the old owl crow fight
which started in his throat
and went out across the bottoms

> *caw caw caw*
> *who-who*
> *who-whoo*
> *whoooooo*
> *whoooooo*

Sending the message
that a bunch of crows had found an owl
had disturbed his daytime sleep
had set upon him
and were diving dodging driving

the old enemy from his resting place.
It was more than crows could resist
and they came to the sound
looking for the battle
eager to claim a piece of the kill
but Mr. C. W. was the killer
stepping from his hiding place
still cawing and hooting
right up until he pulled the triggers
always dropping two
black among the green leaves.

One time he almost missed
and a crow fell with a broken wing
and he took it home
and put it in his henhouse
with a splint on its wing
and fed it and trained it
to sit on his hand.
Then he took it to the woods and let it caw
while he hooted
a Judas crow
calling its friends and family
to die two at a time
one from each barrel.

One time I asked him why
and he said they eat corn in the field
and that seemed reason enough
but he fed his Judas crow corn from the crib
And when the crow died
old Mr. C.W. didn't come around much
but we would see him at the store
stocking up on shotgun shells
or hear him cawing and hooting
down in the woods
calling in crows
and killing them two at a time.

◆ ◆ ◆

Fox Hunt

Is it true the fox loves the hunt
and plays games with the pack
while men squat around fires
and boys stand back and slap mosquitoes
or sleep on a car seat
or on the shelf of a coupe
or in a pickup
and wait for the chase?

> *Hike there! Speak to em!*
> *Speak to em!*

And do the dogs know they should not catch him
but just bark
and try to get ahead of the others

> *Old Peaches is moving up, Lester*
> *about in the middle*

and let their masters know
so they can talk about it
and spit in the fire and laugh at the sound
and teach the boys to love a dog's mouth
and know it as it comes out of the bottoms
through the pines?

> *Old Phoebe has kindly of a yodel,*
> *don't she*
> *a real pretty mouth*

And do the men think on the mystery of it
for boys bred hunters
to run to the crossing place
sucking the wet night air
pointing the flashlight and not a gun
for the shining of that red and white tail

> *Go to ground any time he wants to*
> *but he don't look tired yet*

Then light another fire and listen
as it settles on them
how foxes and other things
move easily through dark woods
leading their chase and going to ground
only at their pleasure?

◆ ◆ ◆

The Copperhead According to Mother Ruth
(for her grandchildren)

Get him with a hoe
but don't step on the head
He'll bite you
even dead

Remember Aunt Callie
between heel and tree
he bit and ran
from Uncle Vee

Look in brushpiles
circle them wide
he's their color
and he'll hide

He's God's creature
but it's also true
you must do unto him
before he does unto you

◆ ◆ ◆

Christmas

I

We always talked about white Christmases
but there rarely was one.
They were mostly gray and wet cold
that cut through our mackinaws
when we went for the tree
Preacher mule pulling the sled
down through the pasture and across a cotton field
with some unpicked still hanging ragged white on the stalks
to the bottom of cane and honeysuckle and sawbriars
and a few patches of cedars or pines.
We'd look at every tree

>   *We could cut the top*
>   *out of a big'un, Uncle Vee*

Then we'd tie it to the sled
and Preacher would pull it up the hill
his breath smoking from his nostrils
some of us running ahead
to tell the coming of the best Christmas tree

II

In the kitchen Allie Jo and Aunt Callie popped corn
from a little patch Uncle Vee planted every year
on the edge of a feed corn field
(and sometimes the August sun was so hot
it would pop on the cob)
and strung it on sewing thread
coiling it on the table
like a snake of popcorn
And we'd try a handful
complaining at the taste

>   *We didn't put no salt on it*
>   *'less you boys eat it all*
>   *'fore we get it strung*

Uncle Vee mounted the tree on some scrap boards
and set it upright in a corner
across the room away from the fireplace

One spark boys
and the whole house'd go

When the popcorn snake was wrapped in and around the tree
we tied ribbons on the branches
and hung last year's Christmas cards
Aunt Callie had saved
most with a manger scene
or a picture of stained glass windows
(which we would see only years later
in city churches
where the people had money
and the preachers thought stained glass was important).
Sometimes we stuck cotton balls in the tree
and one year Aunt Callie tried making snow
from Ivory Snow like in a magazine
but it dried and crumbled on the floor
and Uncle Vee said it was more mess than it was worth.
We blew balloons and tied them like colored balls
and when the pine needles popped them
we would suck the rubber pieces
into little balloons in our mouths
then twist and tie them
making the tree shabby with colored rags of rubber

III

Cousin Hamer had a crystal radio with earphones
because he was blind from when one of his brothers
hit him in the eye with a sweetgum ball

Them boys was meaner'n house dogs
but they didn't mean no harm

and we took turns listening to Christmas carols
from big churches off somewhere
probably Memphis.
He would tune and tune the radio
and pass the earphones around
until the batteries got weak
and the music sounded farther and farther away
Then we'd sing for him
and have a prayer
and go home
always blowing out the lamps before we left
because he didn't need the light

IV

We called Brasil nuts niggertoes
and we called chocolate covered creams niggertoes
and we got both kinds at Christmas
and tangerines
like oranges that were easy to peel
Stockings
big boot socks full of tangerines
and pecans and jawbreakers and sometimes a grapefruit.
Uncle Vee always saved the biggest ham in the smokehouse
salt cured and smoked and two years hanging
and Aunt Callie would soak it and simmer it all day
then chill it in the coldest corner of the bedroom
farthest from the fireplace
and Uncle Vee would sharpen the butcher knife
until we'd be scared to touch it
and slice the ham so thin we could almost see through it

> *Mind grabbing those scraps like that boys*
> *good way to lose a finger*

We put the ham in biscuits
not fat dough biscuits but thin crusty ones
baked special for Christmas.
The rest of the food was the same as any Sunday
only there was more of it
maybe three kinds of meat
and more cakes and pies and teacakes
and we got to eat between meals

V

Morning was always early but Christmas was extra early
the first up stoking the fire and getting in wood
not complaining of the cold floor or the early chores.
Santa would have eaten his teacakes and drunk his coffee
and left us clothes mostly
a belt or gloves or rubber boots
or flowered shirts and dresses
from feed sack patterns we had seen in the feed shed
but never questioned that reindeer feed
must also come in printed sacks.
One year there was a mold for lead soldiers
and a little melting pot and a bar of lead

> *Now you got to be extra careful*
> *with that hot lead boys*

And we made the same soldiers
and killed them in battle
and melted them down
and made them again
until we burned out the mold

VI

Everybody acted happier
except when we prayed that all the soldier boys
would be home from the war by next Christmas.
We went to church and sang carols
and sometimes acted out the baby Jesus story
using old sheets and robes to be wise men and shepherds.
And the preacher said
wouldn't it be nice if we could keep
the spirit of Christmas all year long
And we thought it would be nice
and told ourselves we'd try

◆ ◆ ◆

Misplaced Woodsman

I see a woodsman in the parking lot
stopping amidst the cars
as if he did not have to stop
studying the stars
as if he did not know his direction now
smelling the air
as if seeking the wetness of a yonder river.

The woodsman's mind moves easily through the trees
barefoot across the slick bottom
bending poles and snapping sawbriars
leading the lost fishermen
out of the river
out of the storm.

I see a woodsman in the parking lot
turning at the car
as if waving the hunters ahead
bracing on the door
as if mounting a flat bed pickup
pressing and twisting
as if he needed no new legs.

The woodsman's mind cuts himself from under the fallen tree
hefting the McCullough with a sure hand
lifting limb by limb
making finally a crutch
complaining later that he should have stayed
until the job was done.

I see a woodsman in the parking lot
leaning as if there were no rubber tip cane
shading his eyes as if the pigeons
were a string of high geese
cupping his ear
as if expecting sudden wingbeats
or the bays of a far-off pack.

The woodsman's mind hears one voice among the hounds
figuring where the pack will cross
laughing at the red and white tail
sleeping later like the fox
the chase over
calmly gone to ground.

I see a woodsman in the parking lot
watching the sky for darkening clouds
as if no dams had stopped the floods
as if there were no beans where the water had been
measuring the horizon
as if the safe route were his to choose
as if no highways cut through the ancient hills
as if there were no air conditioned cab
no four wheel drive
no CB radio
As if there were none of those things to make life easy
without a woodsman.

◆ ◆ ◆

This photograph was taken in South Carolina in 1943; the men playing checkers were in Georgia, 1939; and the sleeping dog, also in Georgia, escaped the sun in 1941; but the quiet spirit of a southern small town summer transcends time and place.
Photos: Library of Congress.

Mr. Sanford Hale,
opposite page, was
a hunter, farmer,
husband, father,
grandfather, friend,
all those things
which make a life.
But perhaps he
was proudest of
his role in the
Philadelphia Baptist
church, near Oxford,
Mississippi, where he
was deacon and
songleader. He and
his singers traveled
many a dusty road
to all-day singings
in the north
Mississippi hills.
In the top
photograph, he was
attending Philadelphia
church's centennial.
These photos are
from a family
album.
The church above
was in North
Carolina in 1939,
but it could have
been in a thousand
different places,
with its twin doors,
one for each aisle,
and its ubiquitous
clusters of men on
one side, talking
farming, weather, and
politics, and the women
talking cooking,
canning and children.
Photo: Library of
Congress.

*Left: A church
benefit dinner
in Kentucky
in 1940. The
ladies of the
church
baked for days
then gathered
to urge everyone
else to eat.*

Left and above,
another dinner on
the grounds in
Kentucky, with
the ladies peeling
and slicing
home-grown tomatoes.
Under the trees
the places are
set, awaiting the
singing, the praying,
and the eating.
Photo: Library of
Congress.

This congregation
of a Primitive
Baptist church in
Kentucky
gathered at the
river in 1940
for a baptism.
Photo: Library
of Congress

III. Flashbacks

• • •

Photo: Library of Congress

Progress

I

In the browning picture the whole town sits
man woman and child
smiling from the stump
workmen with axes and saws to the side.
How had it looked
a cypress big as a town's population
and tall as Poff Hill
its round top knees like children wading
all lamps and coffee tables now
and it confined as pecky paneling?

II

In the black dawn where the big trees had been
we waded mud for a mile
to the flat bottom boat
another mile on the water and we were not yet to the river
or beyond to the deep slash
of the duck, beaver, muskrat, egret, snake
their place gone now to beans
waist high across the bottomland
making forty bushels on an acre of memories

III

Boiling okra slimey stews and singing in Ira's pasture
cajuns channeled the Tippah and drained the old run
their big machines ripping the willows and straightening the bends
bringing land where the flood was
pushing out the cottonmouths and beaver dams
pushing out the bream the sweet willow catfish
pushing out the mysteries of the deep slash
proving it was mud and water after all

◆ ◆ ◆

Genealogy

You are
in these hills
who you were and who you will become
and not just who you are

> *She was a McKinstry*
> *and his mother was a Smith*

And the listeners nod
at what the combination will produce
those generations to come
of thievery or honesty
of heathens or Christians
of slovenly men or working

> *'Course her mother was a Sprayberry*

And the new name rises
to the shaking of heads
the tightening of lips
the widening of eyes

> *And his daddy's mother was a McIlhenney*

Oh god a McIlhenney
and silence prays for the unborn children
those little McKinstry Smith Sprayberry McIlhenneys

> *Her daddy was no count and her daddy's daddy was no count*

Old Brother Jim Goff said it
when Mary Allen was pregnant

> *Might's well send that chile*
> *to the penitentiary soons he's born*
> *gonna end up there anyway*

But that lineage could also forgive
with benign expectation
of transgressions to come

> *'Course, what do you expect*
> *his granddaddy was a Wilkins*

or

> *The Whitsells are a little crazy*
> *but they generally don't beat up nobody outside the family*

or

> *You can't expect much work out of a Latham*
> *but they won't steal from you*

In other times and other places
there are new families and new names

> *He's ex P&G*
> *out of Benton and Bowles*
> *and was brand management with Colgate*

And listeners sip Dewar's and soda or puff New True Lights
and know how people will do things
they are expected to do
New fathers spring up and new sons and grandsons
always in jeopardy of leaving the family

> *Watch young Dillard*
> *if he can work for Burton he's golden*
> *but he could be out tomorrow*

And new marriages are bartered for old-fashioned reasons

> *If you want a direct marketing guy*
> *get a headhunter after someone at Time Inc.*

Through it all
communities new and old watch and judge and make sure
the names are in order
and everyone understands

◆　◆　◆

Off Again
(Reflections of the Modern Traveler)

Off again
in all directions
like a chicken with his head cut off
like a blind dog in a meat packing house
like all those things
the old people would say
if they could see me now.

It was the same
plowing a mule geeing and hawing
in the hot wet sun
sweating a spot on the porch
at dinnertime
then off again
to the slanting red fields.

It was the same
hauling fertilizer to Memphis
stopping at the Toddle House
or the Villanova where a pork chop
cost more then a steak ought to
then off again
down the black top.

It was the same
on a Greyhound bus down '78
squeezing among the uniforms and hip flasks
walking the last ten miles
past the red schoolhouse and the soapstone gully
then off again
after the cotton was picked and to the gin.

Now it's all directions at once
with an air travel card
and a carry on bag
writing a speech working a budget
sweating a meeting chewing a tums
like a chicken with his head cut off
like a blind dog in a meat packing house.

◆ ◆ ◆

Urban Flashback

Sitting somber in chauffeured cars,
surrounded by music and other people's stares,
wondering,
if I could go back
to laughing summer days
in '37 Chevrolet flat bed trucks
on dust-choking gravel roads.

Nodding with concern in padded conference rooms,
breathing cigar smoke and unscented deodorants,
wondering,
who here could recognize me
as I chopped at the threatening grass
and loosened the red sand soil
around the desperate cotton.

Smiling through dim rooms and light talk,
sipping something chic and soda,
wondering,
which of these ladies would bring
a covered dish and a quart of tea
to set among the prayers and songs
on the dinner grounds in the pine grove.

◆ ◆ ◆

Dialogue with the Past

What are you doing here
in this conference room
out of the cotton fields and red dust
looking over the coffee and pads
lined yellow and legal size
pretending to be a company man?
What do you expect me to think
with your country church and preacher man rightness
nodding at the plan
smiling at the chart
acting like the profit margins make a damn
when I know where you come from?
Who do you think you're kidding
the cowshit just off your shoes
not far enough from overalls
to be happy in a collar
with GQ in the briefcase
a charge at Saks
and your grandfather restless in the cemetery
every time the closet opens?

Wait wait
I'm the same and it is too
and nothing changes but the words
When the CEO shuffles his feet
in their Italian leather loafers
and calls for further study
and appoints a task force
it's one of the county supervisors
in overalls and brogans
kicking the dust and saying
well fellers sometimes I think, well
then again I just don't know
And everybody goes off and thinks about it some more

But what are you trying to prove
when you didn't have a pot to pee in
or a window to throw it out of
when the roof leaked and the rats came in
and you looking now to shelter
your money as well as yourself?

Only that I still want what I wanted
when you cut through the shit
to do to get to hang on to something
and I only made the trade
country church for conference room
deacons for directors
and chicken in the pot for a few shares of stock

◆ ◆ ◆

Smells of Life on Greyhound Buses During World War II

There was a salty ham one time
a prize from the country
during meat rationing.

It covered the sweat
and sour smells
of summer wet undershirts
of field worn overalls
of overdue diapers.

After a while it filled the bus with thoughts of food
and talk of hot biscuits
and butter and red eye gravy

> *You-ever-have-them-big-dough-biscuit*
> *you-could-stick-a-finger-in*
> *and-poke-a-place-to-fill*
> *with-butter-and-jelly?*

Suddenly
that ham made me center of the bus.
There was a staff sergeant
from Camp Currier, Missouri
and the old men called him sojer boy
and he became my friend
and patted the ham and said
he would cure his own again
when he got home from the war.

Sometimes now I wish for that salty smoky ham
but would it fit under the seats of 727s
on stratospheric routes
And could it work its aromatic magic
or would that man made unhuman air
blow it all away?

◆ ◆ ◆

Shades of Gray

Seeing the old gray houses along every back road
lose the fight with vines and weeds
I think of when the old place burned
and shotgun shells went off
as we watched from the big rocks
the fire too hot to get closer
and wondered what Uncle Vee would say
about the place he was born
and his preacher daddy died

> *Never shoulda rented it*
> *now it's gone*

But I think it was better for the old place to burn
full of stuff and not deserted
empty in the woods
good for a picnic pilgrimage and not much else
gray and bent like a crazy old woman
widowed and grandwidowed and great grandwidowed
until no one knows who she is
or how much she meant in those days
how she grunted out children on corn shuck mattresses
and nursed them and wiped them
all the time cooking and washing and hoeing
and weeding and gathering and canning
and waiting for the next baby
all of them gone and their babies gone
her eyes gray and vacant
looking through a screen door
in the old folks' home
still wearing a bonnet to a ragged garden
chopping grass with a hoe so many years sharpened it's now a sliver
living for those times when someone young comes
and surrounds her with life for a while
then goes again
leaving her wondering if there'll be a next time
her life fading grayer and grayer
like a house with vines and brush
with rusty roof and sagging porch
with snakes and rats and coons and birds
but none of the life that gave it a reason to be.

So I'm glad the old place burned when it did
still filled with life
still sheltering love and the coming of children

◆ ◆ ◆

IV. Worship

...

Photos, here and page 76: Library of Congress

Revival Meeting

How many heavy dusty nights
did I sit on wooden pews beside blonde sweating girls
stirring air toward them with funeral parlor fans
while infants slept finger sucking on quilts
and wasps flew heavy winged from lamp to lamp
searching for a place to fall and burn?

How many booming righteous promises of glory
did I ingore for whispered hints of ecstacy
while nervous deacons sun reddened in overalls
shouted self-conscious amens
and pale children pressed scared faces
into their mothers' laps?

How many stanzas of O Lamb of God I Come
did I sing on key and off
squirming with sweat sticking white shirt and khakis
still fanning and feeling that blonde warmth
while preachers pleaded voice catching phrases
and babies sucked late night breasts?

How many big and growing cousins
did I pat on work hardened backs
standing in the car fume night air
watching them twist hand rolled bull durhams into their lips
while bats swept wing dodging through the pole light
and blonde girls took sweat cooling walks?

How many veiled and wrinkled aunts
did I kiss on powdered cheeks
violet bath water smelling but sour
while blonde girls waited
on the pine needle ground beyond the tombstones
ready with slick and heavy tongue kisses?

And how many mornings have I sat
in the still warm and thick air of the empty church
reading the dim communion table carvings
while wasps not crisp dead like the others
flew in and out in and out
finding the lamps unlit and the sun too far away?

◆ ◆ ◆

All Day Singing with Dinner on the Grounds

I

There were old men with ear trumpets
who patted their feet against the rhythm
and sang notes melodious only to themselves
sitting near the front on an aisle
where some young cousin or nephew had led them.
Snuff staining the corners of their mouths
tobacco breath filling the rows around them
they stayed there most of the day
but the rest of us moved in and out
and new groups came
in cars and trucks and yellow school buses

> *Here come*
> *Mr. Sanford Hale*
> *and the Philadelphia singers*

Coming to the singing convention
coming from three or four counties away
on dusty roads over hills and through bottoms
in heat that made the radiators boil
and fresh ironed shirts go damp and wrinkled
in heat that made the britches stick to our legs
when we got up from the hard oak pews.
Coming to sing
in duets and trios and quartets
and some soloists like Miss Ernestine Lee
whose face had the light of God in it
when she sang How Great Thou Art

> *I declare*
> *you can hear Jesus*
> *in her voice*

And some congregation singing
different song leaders from different churches
taking turns

> *Now we gonna ask*
> *Clyde Wyatt of Bethel Baptist*
> *to lead this next one*

And sometimes they'd get up a quartet
from different churches
always discussing who would sing lead and who would sing bass

Now you come on up here Leon
and you too Hamer
and you sing alto Mr. J.W.

And after two or three false starts
they'd sing all the old ones
all the ones everybody knew and heard on the radio
every Sunday morning before church
On the Jericho Road and
Take a Little Walk with Jesus and
My God is Real and
I Saw the Light

Sometimes they'd make all the ladies sing a verse
or all the children
or all the folks over sixty
Then between songs there'd be testimonials
or one of the preachers would lead a prayer
because all the preachers from all the churches came
and led a prayer before the day was over.

II

Late in the morning
by some signal I never saw
the ladies began to leave the church and go to the cars
and get baskets and sacks
and head to the dinnergrounds,
big gray tables under the trees
or sometimes rough lumber nailed between the trees,
and spread starched table cloths
and decide somehow among themselves
where the meat would be
and the vegetables and bread
where to gather the cakes and pies
and jugs of iced tea.
Then someone would let the songleader know
and he'd say that dinner was ready
and everybody would go outside and have another song
and a prayer
then start along the tables
smiling at their neighbors
thanking God for the day
spooning their plates full

Now you boys just keep back
and let them ladies go first

It seemed all the food in the world
fried chicken crisp and soggy
country ham and sausage in biscuits
deviled eggs and creamed corn
and blackeyed peas and okra
and green beans and sliced tomatoes
and corn bread and spoon bread
and all manner of pies and cakes
stacked apple pies and Mississippi mud pies
pound cakes sliced thick with strawberries and cream
big wet banana cakes
and coconut cakes you ate with a spoon.
And the ladies would watch to see
whose dishes got eaten first

> *Miss Nora*
> *you just can't make enough*
> *of them old time buttermilk pies*

and smile and say how this wasn't near as good
as they usually make.

III

Then the singing would start again
with people coming and going
with men and boys standing outside the open windows
rolling cigarettes from little sacks of tobacco
picking their teeth with black gum brushes
and spitting into the red powder dust.
And later in the afternoon
we'd go off into the pines behind the church
and throw rocks
and shoot green plums from our slingshots
and not really listen to the singing any more
but hear it anyway
and the motors starting
and the people getting on the schoolbuses
and our names called when it was time to go.

◆ ◆ ◆

Baptism

He waded into the cold water up to his knees
then across a sandbar and into the current
and turned and called to us
and suddenly the swimming hole was different.
We'd been there for a thousand swims
but it was different
colder maybe
swifter
deeper
surrounded not by boys and girls in swim suits
but by Sunday dressed ladies and coat and tied men
singing

> *Shall we gather at the river*
> *the beautiful the beautiful*
> *river*

And we moved in a line
barefoot and in white shirts and wash pants
the girls in dark colored dresses
which would not show through when they got wet
Across the shallows onto the sandbar
and from there went one at a time
in the name of the father, the son, and the holy ghost
to be put under the water
his arm behind our shoulders
and his hand over our mouth and nose
and our hand on his hand
For only a few seconds but it seemed longer
longer than any time when we had jumped or dropped from a vine
longer than when we swam underwater to scare the girls
longer than we thought we could ever stand
but he pulled us up
and said amen and the people said hallelujah
and our mothers hugged us as we went wet onto the bank.

Then he came out of the water
and we sang On Jordan's Stormy Banks I Stand
and he lifted his arms over us
all shivering there
the water draining from our pants cuffs
dresses clinging to the girls' legs

And said some words
about our sins washed away
and cleansed in the blood
and born again
And told us we were saved
and would go to heaven
and have life everlasting
and many other important things
we remembered for a long time.

◆   ◆   ◆

V. Death

• • •

Death in the Family

I

People hug us and cry
and pray we'll be strong
and know we'll see her again someday
And we nod and they pat and rub
reassuring her to heaven

> *She's with Jesus now*
> *no suffering where she is*

Then sit on hard benches and sing
of precious memories how they linger
and farther along we'll understand it

> *Cheer up my brother*
> *We're not forgotten*

The preacher studies his Bible and stares at the ceiling
and the song leader in his blue funeral suit sweats
and strokes the air
with a callused hand

> *We'll understand it*
> *all bye and bye*

And powdered and rosy cheeked
Miss Anne sleeps in an open coffin
the children standing tiptoe to see through the flowers
but scared to go near and drawing back when lifted
And the choir brings a balm in Gilead
and a roll is called up yonder

> *When the trumpet of the lord shall sound*
> *and time shall be no more*

And big men shake heads white at the hat line
while women weep and flutter air with palm leaf fans
And later we stand amidst the stones
by the mound of red clay
our eyes wet against the sun
and listen to preachers and mockingbirds
and the 23rd Psalm

II

Men stand uneasy in ties
and nod their hats to ladies
and kick gravel with shoes too tight
and talk about life

> *Nobody no better'n Miss Anne*
> *No Sir*
> *No Sir*

Smoking bull durhams around the porch
shaking their heads to agree
and sucking wind through their teeth

> *Never let you go thirsty*
> *bring a jugga tea to the field*
> *ever day*

They open doors for us and look at the ground
as if by not seeing our faces they become invisible
There are not enough chores
so three draw well water
and two get the mail
and four feed the dogs
and the rest chop wood
and wish for something to say

> *Lester broke his arm one time*
> *and Miss Anne plowed that mule*
> *like a man*
> *put in the whole crop*

And they talk of crops and plowing
of rain and sun and flood and drought
The seasons passing in memory
marking changes in years and lives
that men remember at times
when there's nothing to say

III

Ladies come with sad faces
and baskets of sweets
teacakes, pecan pies, puddings, memories
and we choose and they serve
telling stories and god blessing the children

I declare that Miss Anne
was the sweetest Christian person
in the world

Saying all the things to be said
doing all the things to be done
like orderly spirits
freshening beds from the grieving night
poking up fires gone cold
filling the table and sideboard
then gathering there to urge and cajole
as if the dead rest easier on our full stomachs

Lord how Miss Anne would have loved that country ham

No sadness so great it cannot be fed away
by the insistent spirits

That banana cake is her very own recipe
I remember how she loved my spoon bread
She canned the berries in this cobbler

And suddenly we are transformed
and eat and smile and thank you
and the ladies nod and know they have done well again
in time of need
And the little girls watch and learn
And we forget the early spring cemetery
and the church with precious memories
and farther along we do understand it
the payments and repayments
of all the ladies that were and are
and we pray ever will be. Amen

◆ ◆ ◆

Prayer for a Country Preacher

Oh God
let him go dreaming when he goes
let him go preaching a revival meeting
with the congregation eager beyond discomfort
on a wet and insect laden night

let him go singing bass
on a Sunday morning
his head above the others
his voice bringing power beyond
power in the blood

let him go walking the river bottom
leading the lost fishermen through the storm
breaking saplings to mark the trail

let him go wading the shallows
his boots sucking mud in the dawn
calling the green headed mallard
shooting quick and sure

       Not bad for a country preacher

let him go praying
at a table of summer Sunday food
fried chicken and sliced tomatoes
and peas and cornbread and tea
with his family around him
like disciples

Oh God if he must go
let him go dreaming

◆ ◆ ◆

Death Message

How long have I waited
for this late night phone ringing?
To come awake knowing
and to lie awake thinking
And it came on a night
when I heard a far-off train
calling in two tones
letting everyone know it was
moving on down the line.

Far-off trains and dying people
roll together through my life
as if no one in Mississippi
can die without a mourning train
to start the dogs howling
to set loose all the sounds
of a world turned sad.

In that night and dawning
unreal rafters reveal themselves
above the bed
a thin memory of rough sawn boards
and dawns under a tin roof.
Then a jet whines
no mourning train but a space machine
returning me to a lifetime ago.

◆ ◆ ◆

Against All Those Desperate Prayers

Against all those desperate prayers
whispered in airplanes
and hospital corridors
Against all those deals and bargains
of new beginnings and new behaviors I thought God
could not afford to pass up
Against all the wild promises
he died anyway.

◆ ◆ ◆